THE
FOCUS
JOURNAL

JOLIE RASHAWN

www.jolierashawn.com
Copyright 2020
ISBN: 9781660275359

This is a publication of AB Enterprise LLC

SPECIAL EVENTS

MONTH/EVENT	MONTH/EVENT

MONTH/EVENT	MONTH/EVENT

MONTH/EVENT	MONTH/EVENT

SPECIAL EVENTS

MONTH/EVENT

MONTH/EVENT

MONTH/EVENT

MONTH/EVENT

MONTH/EVENT

MONTH/EVENT

MONTH _____

S	M	T	W	TH	F	S

NOTES

THINGS TO DO THIS WEEK

MONDAY

_____
_____
_____
_____

TUESDAY

_____
_____
_____
_____

WEDNESDAY

_____
_____
_____
_____

THURSDAY

_____
_____
_____
_____

FRIDAY

SATURDAY

SUNDAY

PRAYER LIST

Chapter 1:
LEARNING YOURSELF
"No one can tell you who you are!"

Who are you?

_____
_____
_____
_____

What makes you happy?

_____
_____
_____
_____

What drives you?

_____
_____
_____
_____

WEEK 1

I Peter 2:10: *"Once you were not a people, but now you are the people of God; once you had not received mercy, but now you have received mercy"*.

Mediate and Write your thoughts about this scripture.

___
___
___
___
___
___
___
___
___
___
___
___
___
___
___

THINGS TO DO THIS WEEK

MONDAY

TUESDAY

WEDNESDAY

THURSDAY

FRIDAY

SATURDAY

SUNDAY

PRAYER LIST

WEEK 2

Psalm 32:8 I will instruct you and teach you in the way which you shall go.

Mediate and Write your thoughts about this scripture.

_____

_____

_____

_____

_____

_____

_____

_____

_____

_____

_____

_____

_____

_____

_____

THINGS TO DO THIS WEEK

MONDAY

TUESDAY

WEDNESDAY

THURSDAY

FRIDAY

SATURDAY

SUNDAY

PRAYER LIST

WEEK 3

Philippians 4:9 Do the things which you learned, received, heard, and saw in me, and the God of peace will be with you

Mediate and Write your thoughts about this scripture.

_____

_____

_____

_____

_____

_____

_____

_____

_____

_____

_____

_____

_____

_____

THINGS TO DO THIS WEEK

MONDAY

TUESDAY

WEDNESDAY

THURSDAY

FRIDAY

___

SATURDAY

___

SUNDAY

___

PRAYER LIST

WEEK 4

Philippians 4:9 Therefore exhort one another, and build each other up, even as ye also do.

Mediate and Write your thoughts about this scripture.

MONTH

S	M	T	W	TH	F	S

NOTES

THINGS TO DO THIS WEEK

MONDAY

_____
_____
_____

TUESDAY

_____
_____
_____

WEDNESDAY

_____
_____
_____

THURSDAY

_____
_____
_____

FRIDAY

_____
_____
_____
_____

SATURDAY

_____
_____
_____
_____

SUNDAY

_____
_____
_____
_____

PRAYER LIST

_____
_____
_____
_____
_____
_____
_____
_____

Chapter 2:
SELF WORTH
"It's not going to be easy, but it's worth it."

What do you mean to you?

_____
_____
_____
_____

How valuable is what you have to offer?

_____
_____
_____
_____

How do others value you?

_____
_____
_____
_____

WEEK 1

Matthew 13:46 Who having found one pearl of great price, he went and sold all that he had and bought it.

Mediate and Write your thoughts about this scripture.

_____

_____

_____

_____

_____

_____

_____

_____

_____

_____

_____

_____

_____

_____

THINGS TO DO THIS WEEK

MONDAY

_____
_____
_____
_____

TUESDAY

_____
_____
_____
_____

WEDNESDAY

_____
_____
_____
_____

THURSDAY

_____
_____
_____
_____

FRIDAY

SATURDAY

SUNDAY

PRAYER LIST

WEEK 2

Philippians 4:13 I can do all things through Christ who strengthens me.

Mediate and Write your thoughts about this scripture.

_____

_____

_____

_____

_____

_____

_____

_____

_____

_____

_____

_____

_____

_____

_____

THINGS TO DO THIS WEEK

MONDAY

_____
_____
_____
_____

TUESDAY

_____
_____
_____
_____

WEDNESDAY

_____
_____
_____
_____

THURSDAY

_____
_____
_____
_____

FRIDAY

SATURDAY

SUNDAY

PRAYER LIST

WEEK 3

Proverbs 31:25 Strength and dignity are clothing. She laughs at the time to come.

Mediate and Write your thoughts about this scripture.

THINGS TO DO THIS WEEK

MONDAY

TUESDAY

WEDNESDAY

THURSDAY

FRIDAY

SATURDAY

SUNDAY

PRAYER LIST

WEEK 4

Romans 5:8 But God commends his own love towards us, in that while we were yet sinners, Christ died for us.

Mediate and Write your thoughts about this scripture.

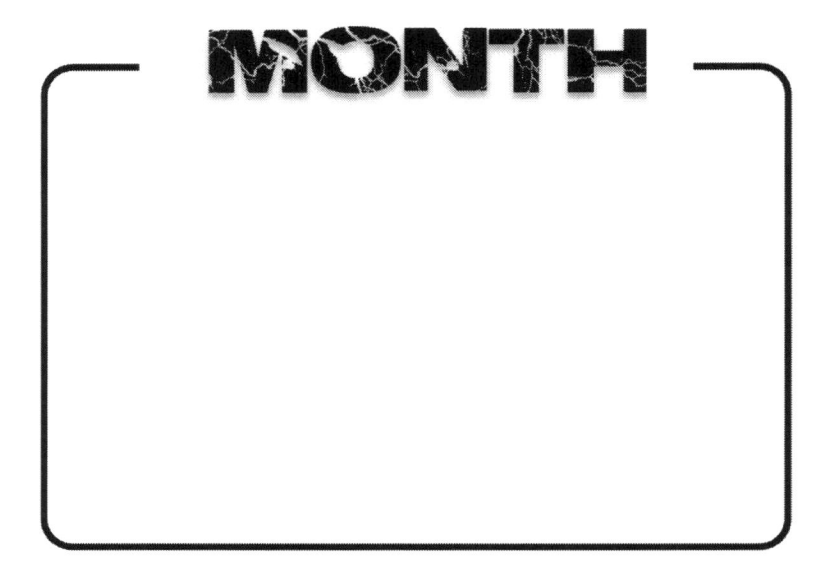

MONTH

MONTH

S	M	T	W	TH	F	S

NOTES

THINGS TO DO THIS WEEK

MONDAY

TUESDAY

WEDNESDAY

THURSDAY

FRIDAY

SATURDAY

SUNDAY

PRAYER LIST

Chapter 3:
SACRIFICE
"Don't even start if you don't plan to give it your all and go all the way."

Is there anything in your life that you consider toxic?

_____

_____

_____

_____

Are you willing to do Late Nights/Early Mornings?

_____

_____

_____

_____

What does your time management look like?

_____

_____

_____

_____

WEEK 1

Ephesians 5:2 Walk in love, even as Christ also loved us and gave himself for us, an offering and a sacrifice to God for a sweet-smelling fragrance.

Mediate and Write your thoughts about this scripture.

_____

_____

_____

_____

_____

_____

_____

_____

_____

_____

_____

_____

_____

_____

THINGS TO DO THIS WEEK

MONDAY

_____
_____
_____
_____

TUESDAY

_____
_____
_____
_____

WEDNESDAY

_____
_____
_____
_____

THURSDAY

_____
_____
_____
_____

FRIDAY

SATURDAY

SUNDAY

PRAYER LIST

WEEK 2

Proverbs 21:3 To do righteousness and justice is more acceptable to the Lord than sacrifice.

Mediate and Write your thoughts about this scripture.

_____

_____

_____

_____

_____

_____

_____

_____

_____

_____

_____

_____

_____

_____

_____

_____

THINGS TO DO THIS WEEK

MONDAY

TUESDAY

WEDNESDAY

THURSDAY

FRIDAY

SATURDAY

SUNDAY

PRAYER LIST

WEEK 3

1 john 1:7 But if we walk in the light as he is in the light, we have fellowship with him one another and the blood of Christ the Messiah, his son, cleanses us from all sin.

Mediate and Write your thoughts about this scripture.

_____
_____
_____
_____
_____
_____
_____
_____
_____
_____
_____
_____
_____
_____
_____
_____

THINGS TO DO THIS WEEK

MONDAY

___

TUESDAY

___

WEDNESDAY

___

THURSDAY

FRIDAY

SATURDAY

SUNDAY

PRAYER LIST

WEEK 4

John 15:13 Greater love has no one than this, to lay down one's life for ones friend.

Mediate and Write your thoughts about this scripture.

_____

_____

_____

_____

_____

_____

_____

_____

_____

_____

_____

_____

_____

_____

_____

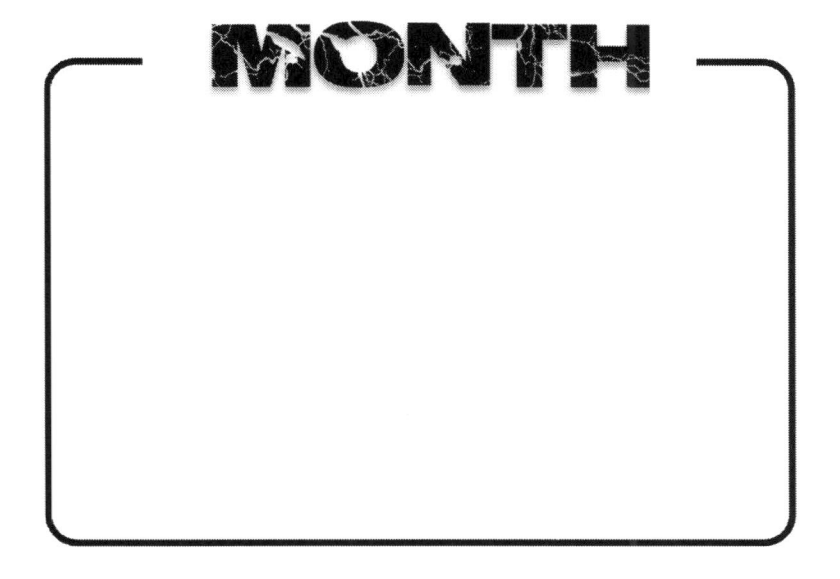

MONTH

MONTH _____

S	M	T	W	TH	F	S

NOTES

THINGS TO DO THIS WEEK

MONDAY

TUESDAY

WEDNESDAY

THURSDAY

FRIDAY

SATURDAY

SUNDAY

PRAYER LIST

Chapter 4:
CLEANSING

""You must take care if the most magnificent machine you have...YOU"

Write down your toxic thinking

_____

_____

How is your Self Care?

_____

_____

What is your focus on positive thinking?

_____

_____

How can you keep God close to your heart?

_____

_____

_____

WEEK 1

Psalms 56:8 You count my wandering, you put my tears in your container. Aren't they in your book?

Mediate and Write your thoughts about this scripture.

_____
_____
_____
_____
_____
_____
_____
_____
_____
_____
_____
_____
_____
_____

THINGS TO DO THIS WEEK

MONDAY

_____
_____
_____

TUESDAY

_____
_____
_____

WEDNESDAY

_____
_____
_____

THURSDAY

_____
_____
_____

FRIDAY

SATURDAY

SUNDAY

PRAYER LIST

WEEK 2

2 Corinthians 7:1 Having therefore these promises, beloved, let's cleanse ourselves from all defilement of flesh and spirit, perfecting holiness in the fear of God.

Mediate and Write your thoughts about this scripture.

THINGS TO DO THIS WEEK

MONDAY

TUESDAY

WEDNESDAY

THURSDAY

FRIDAY

SATURDAY

SUNDAY

PRAYER LIST

WEEK 3

Psalms 51:10 Create in me a clean heart, O God. Renew a right spirit within me.

Mediate and Write your thoughts about this scripture.

THINGS TO DO THIS WEEK

MONDAY

TUESDAY

WEDNESDAY

THURSDAY

FRIDAY

SATURDAY

SUNDAY

PRAYER LIST

WEEK 4

James 4:8 Draw near to God, and He will draw near to you. Cleanse your hands, you sinners. Purify your hearts, you double minded.

Mediate and Write your thoughts about this scripture.

_____

_____

_____

_____

_____

_____

_____

_____

_____

_____

_____

_____

_____

_____

_____

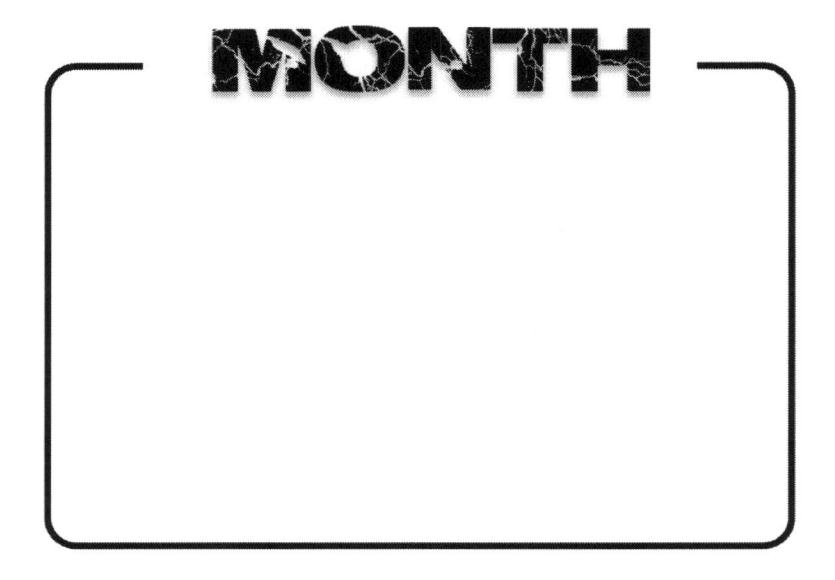

MONTH

MONTH _____

S	M	T	W	TH	F	S

NOTES

THINGS TO DO THIS WEEK

MONDAY

TUESDAY

WEDNESDAY

THURSDAY

FRIDAY

SATURDAY

SUNDAY

PRAYER LIST

Chapter 5:
INVESTMENT
"Make investments to create a second chance."

Invest in yourself!

_____
_____
_____
_____

Invest time in your business!

_____
_____
_____
_____

Invest in others!

_____
_____
_____
_____

WEEK 1

Matthew 6:21 for where your treasure is, there your heart will be also.

Mediate and Write your thoughts about this scripture.

_____
_____
_____
_____
_____
_____
_____
_____
_____
_____
_____
_____
_____
_____
_____
_____

THINGS TO DO THIS WEEK

MONDAY

TUESDAY

WEDNESDAY

THURSDAY

FRIDAY

SATURDAY

SUNDAY

PRAYER LIST

WEEK 2

Proverbs 15:22 where there is no counsel, plans fail; but in multitude of counselors they are established

Mediate and Write your thoughts about this scripture.

THINGS TO DO THIS WEEK

MONDAY

___
___
___

TUESDAY

___
___
___

WEDNESDAY

___
___
___

THURSDAY

___
___
___

FRIDAY

SATURDAY

SUNDAY

PRAYER LIST

WEEK 3

Proverbs 19:2 It isn't good to have zeal without knowledge, nor being hasty with ones feet and missing the way.

Mediate and Write your thoughts about this scripture.

THINGS TO DO THIS WEEK

MONDAY

___

___

___

___

TUESDAY

___

___

___

___

WEDNESDAY

___

___

___

___

THURSDAY

___

___

___

___

FRIDAY

SATURDAY

SUNDAY

PRAYER LIST

WEEK 4

Proverbs 28:26 One who trusts in himself is a fool; but one who walks in wisdom is kept safe.

Mediate and Write your thoughts about this scripture.

MONTH

MONTH _____

S	M	T	W	TH	F	S

NOTES

THINGS TO DO THIS WEEK

MONDAY

TUESDAY

WEDNESDAY

THURSDAY

FRIDAY

SATURDAY

SUNDAY

PRAYER LIST

Chapter 6:
CHANGE YOUR SURROUNDINGS

"If you don't like something, you can always change it, if you can't change it, just change the way you think about it!"

What about your occupation fulfill you?

_____
_____
_____
_____

How are your relationships helping you?

_____
_____
_____
_____

How are your friendships add value to your life?

_____
_____
_____
_____

WEEK 1
Psalms 51:10 Create in me a clean heart O God

Mediate and Write your thoughts about this scripture.

THINGS TO DO THIS WEEK

MONDAY

TUESDAY

WEDNESDAY

THURSDAY

FRIDAY

_____
_____
_____
_____

SATURDAY

_____
_____
_____
_____

SUNDAY

_____
_____
_____
_____

PRAYER LIST

WEEK 2

Isaiah 43:19 Behold I will do a new thing.

Mediate and Write your thoughts about this scripture.

THINGS TO DO THIS WEEK

MONDAY

TUESDAY

WEDNESDAY

THURSDAY

FRIDAY

SATURDAY

SUNDAY

PRAYER LIST

WEEK 3

2 CORINTHIANS 5:17 Therefore if anyone is in Christ, he is a new creation. The old things have passed away, Behold all things become new

.Mediate and Write your thoughts about this scripture.

_____
_____
_____
_____
_____
_____
_____
_____
_____
_____
_____
_____
_____
_____
_____

THINGS TO DO THIS WEEK

MONDAY

_____
_____
_____
_____

TUESDAY

_____
_____
_____
_____

WEDNESDAY

_____
_____
_____
_____

THURSDAY

_____
_____
_____
_____

FRIDAY

SATURDAY

SUNDAY

PRAYER LIST

WEEK 4

Ezekiel 36:26 I will also give you a new heart and I will put a new spirit in you.

Mediate and Write your thoughts about this scripture.

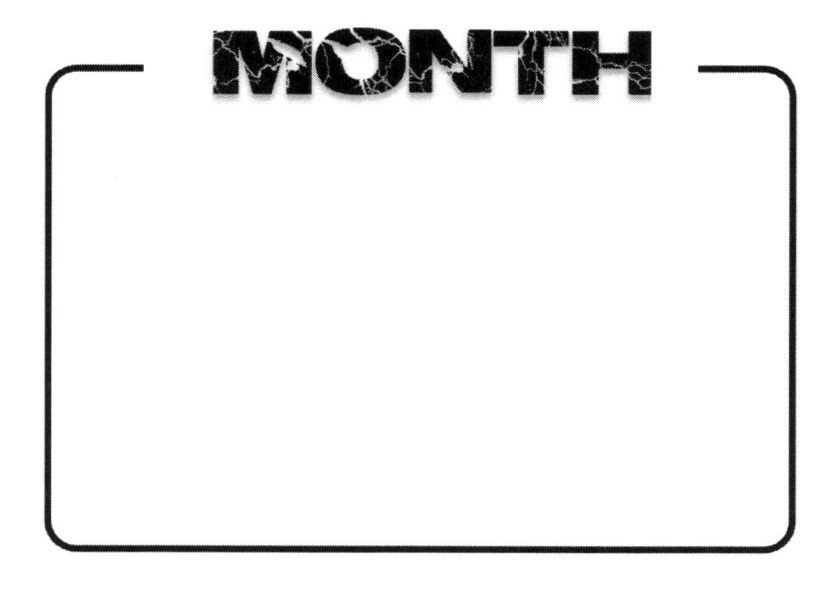

MONTH

MONTH

S	M	T	W	TH	F	S

NOTES

THINGS TO DO THIS WEEK

MONDAY
___
___
___
___

TUESDAY
___
___
___
___

WEDNESDAY
___
___
___
___

THURSDAY
___
___
___
___

FRIDAY

SATURDAY

SUNDAY

PRAYER LIST

Chapter 7:
ORGANIZE
"An hour is earned every minute you spend organizing."

How do you organize your thoughts?

_____
_____
_____

How is your office space organized?

_____
_____
_____

How is your devotion?

_____
_____
_____

How often do you keep your journal/calendar organized?

_____
_____

WEEK 1

Ephesians 4:16 from whom all the body, being fitted and knit together through that which every joint supplies, according to the working in measure of each individual part, makes the body increase to the building up of. Itself in love.

Mediate and Write your thoughts about this scripture.

THINGS TO DO THIS WEEK

MONDAY

___

TUESDAY

___

WEDNESDAY

___

THURSDAY

___

FRIDAY

SATURDAY

SUNDAY

PRAYER LIST

WEEK 2

1 Corinthians 12:28 God has set some in the assembly; first emissaries, second prophets, third teachers, then miracle workers, then gifts of healings, helps, governments, and various kinds of languages.

Mediate and Write your thoughts about this scripture.

_____

_____

_____

_____

_____

_____

_____

_____

_____

_____

_____

_____

_____

_____

THINGS TO DO THIS WEEK

MONDAY

___

TUESDAY

___

WEDNESDAY

___

THURSDAY

___

FRIDAY

SATURDAY

SUNDAY

PRAYER LIST

WEEK 3

Proverbs 10:4 He becomes poor who works with a lazy hand, but the hand of the diligent brings wealth.

Mediate and Write your thoughts about this scripture.

_____

_____

_____

_____

_____

_____

_____

_____

_____

_____

_____

_____

_____

_____

_____

THINGS TO DO THIS WEEK

MONDAY

TUESDAY

WEDNESDAY

THURSDAY

FRIDAY

SATURDAY

SUNDAY

PRAYER LIST

WEEK 4

Ephesians 4:4 Therefore is one body and one Spirit, even as you also were called in one hope of your calling

Mediate and Write your thoughts about this scripture.

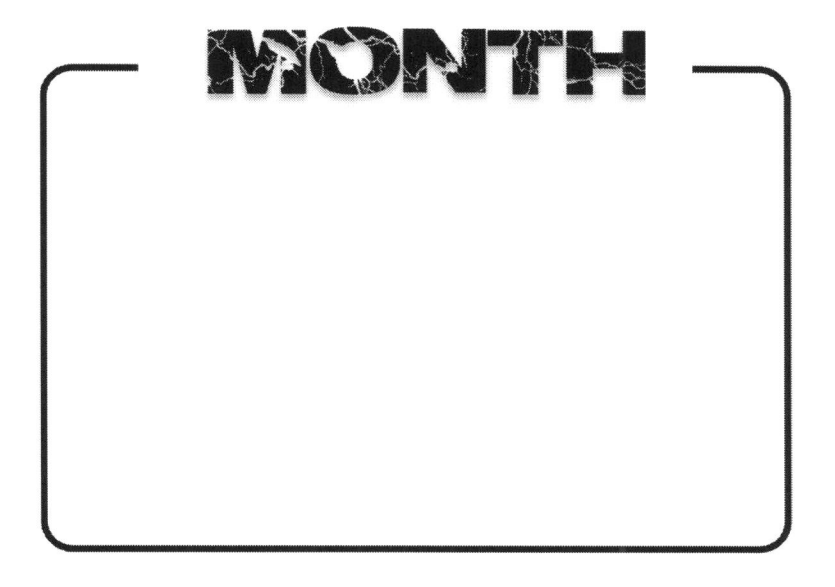

MONTH

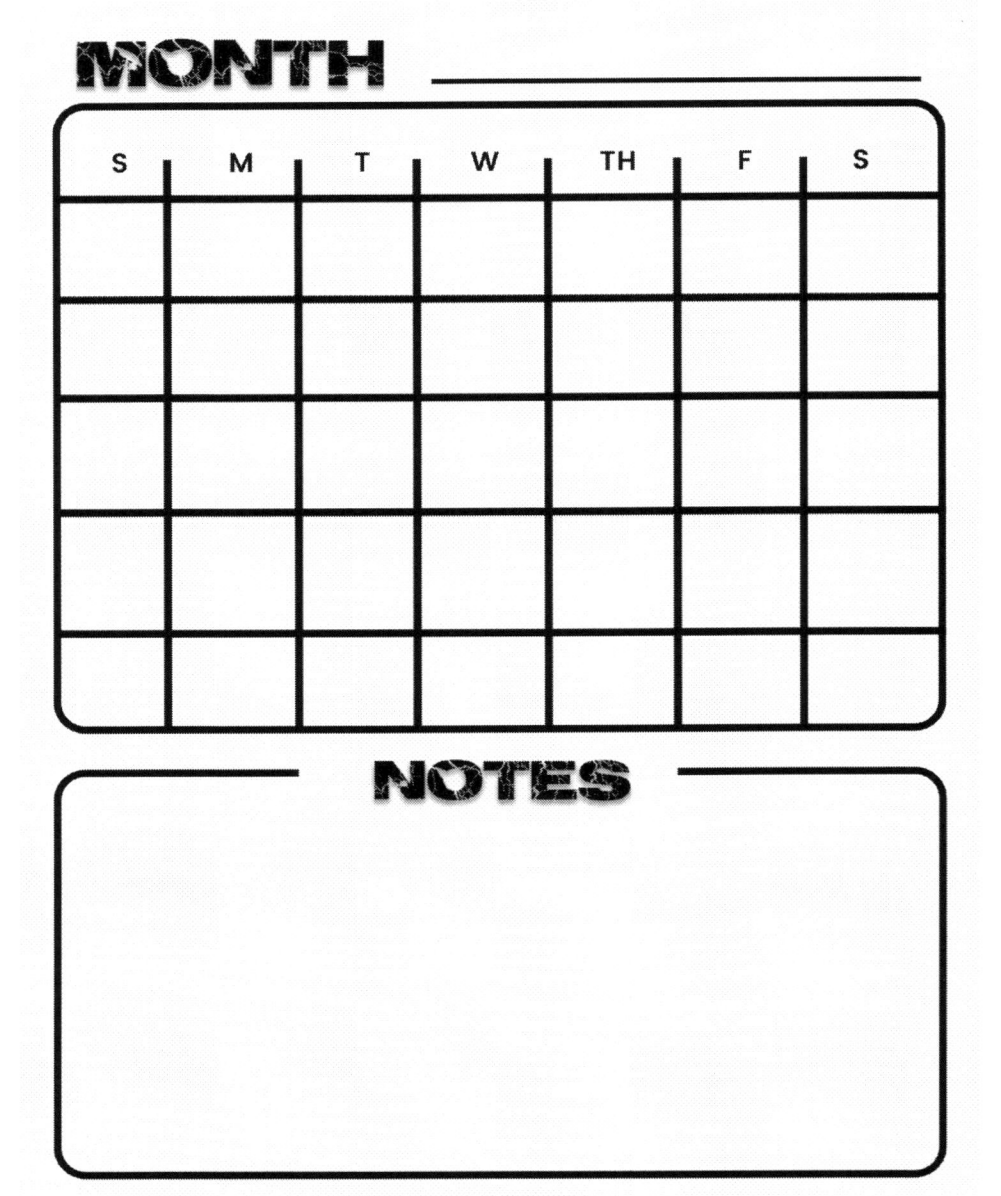

MONTH

S	M	T	W	TH	F	S

NOTES

THINGS TO DO THIS WEEK

MONDAY

TUESDAY

WEDNESDAY

THURSDAY

FRIDAY

SATURDAY

SUNDAY

PRAYER LIST

Chapter 8:
MAKE IT PLAIN
"Think the idea. See the vision. Walk the plan."

Write out everything

_____
_____
_____
_____

Vocalize your ideas

_____
_____
_____
_____

How can you stop second guess yourself?

_____
_____
_____
_____

WEEK 1

Jeremiah 29:11 For I know the thoughts that I think towards you, says the Lord. Thoughts of peace, and not of evil, to give you hope and a future.

Mediate and Write your thoughts about this scripture.

_____
_____
_____
_____
_____
_____
_____
_____
_____
_____
_____
_____
_____
_____

THINGS TO DO THIS WEEK

MONDAY

TUESDAY

WEDNESDAY

THURSDAY

FRIDAY

SATURDAY

SUNDAY

PRAYER LIST

WEEK 2

Numbers 12:6 He said, Now hear my words. If there is a prophet among you, I the Lord will make myself known to him in a vision. I will speak with him in a dream.

Mediate and Write your thoughts about this scripture.

_____

_____

_____

_____

_____

_____

_____

_____

_____

_____

_____

_____

_____

_____

THINGS TO DO THIS WEEK

MONDAY

___
___
___
___

TUESDAY

___
___
___
___

WEDNESDAY

___
___
___
___

THURSDAY

___
___
___
___

FRIDAY

SATURDAY

SUNDAY

PRAYER LIST

WEEK 3

Proverbs 29:18 Where there is no revelation, the people cast off restraint; but one who keeps the Torah is blessed.

Mediate and Write your thoughts about this scripture.

_____
_____
_____
_____
_____
_____
_____
_____
_____
_____
_____
_____
_____

THINGS TO DO THIS WEEK

MONDAY

TUESDAY

WEDNESDAY

THURSDAY

FRIDAY

SATURDAY

SUNDAY

PRAYER LIST

WEEK 4

Habakkuk 2:2-3 The Lord answered me, Write the vision, and make it plain on tablets, that he who runs may read it. For the vision is yet for the appointed time, and it hurries towards the end and wont prove false. Thou it takes time, wait for it, because it will surely come. It won't delay.

Mediate and Write your thoughts about this scripture.

_____

_____

_____

_____

_____

_____

_____

_____

_____

_____

_____

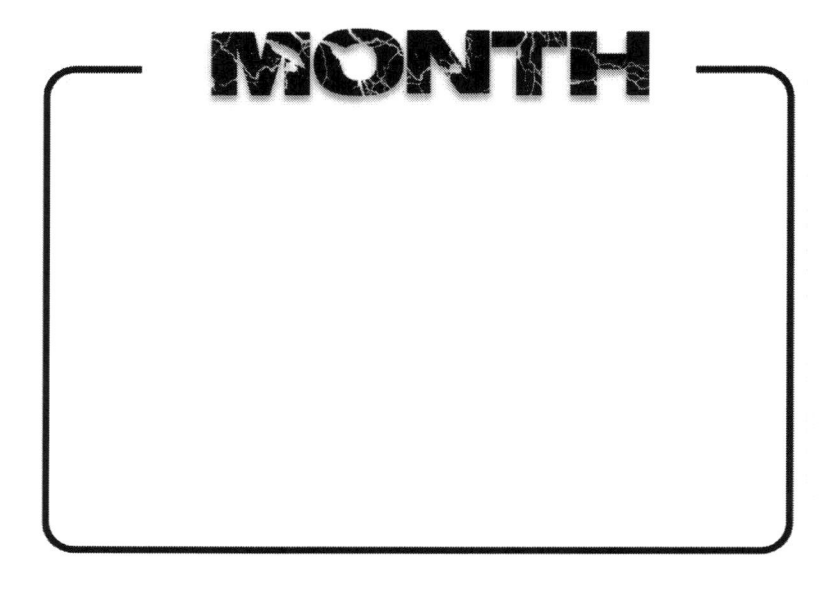

MONTH

MONTH

S	M	T	W	TH	F	S

NOTES

THINGS TO DO THIS WEEK

MONDAY

_____
_____
_____

TUESDAY

_____
_____
_____

WEDNESDAY

_____
_____
_____

THURSDAY

_____
_____
_____

FRIDAY

_____
_____
_____
_____

SATURDAY

_____
_____
_____
_____

SUNDAY

_____
_____
_____
_____

PRAYER LIST

Chapter 9:
ACCEPTANCE

"If you live for people's acceptance, you will perish from their rejection!"

How can you welcome your faults!

_____
_____
_____

How can you acknowledge your failures?

_____
_____
_____

How can you accept responsibility

_____
_____

How can you build a bridge with rejections?

_____
_____

WEEK 1

Philippians 4:6 In nothing be anxious, but in everything, by prayer and petition with thanksgiving, let your requests be made known to God

Mediate and Write your thoughts about this scripture.

_____

_____

_____

_____

_____

_____

_____

_____

_____

_____

_____

_____

_____

_____

THINGS TO DO THIS WEEK

MONDAY

_____
_____
_____
_____

TUESDAY

_____
_____
_____
_____

WEDNESDAY

_____
_____
_____
_____

THURSDAY

_____
_____
_____

FRIDAY

SATURDAY

SUNDAY

PRAYER LIST

WEEK 2

1 peter 3:8 Finally, all of you be like-minded, compassionate, loving as brothers, tender hearted, courteous, not rendering evil for evil or insult for insult; but instead blessing, knowing that you were called to this, that you may inherit a blessing.

Mediate and Write your thoughts about this scripture.

THINGS TO DO THIS WEEK

MONDAY

TUESDAY

WEDNESDAY

THURSDAY

FRIDAY

SATURDAY

SUNDAY

PRAYER LIST

WEEK 3

Proverbs 13:20 One who walks with wise men grows wise, but a companion of fools suffers harm.

Mediate and Write your thoughts about this scripture.

THINGS TO DO THIS WEEK

MONDAY

TUESDAY

WEDNESDAY

THURSDAY

FRIDAY

SATURDAY

SUNDAY

PRAYER LIST

WEEK 4

Romans 8:31 What then shall we say about these things? If God is for us, who can be against us?

Mediate and Write your thoughts about this scripture.

_____
_____
_____
_____
_____
_____
_____
_____
_____
_____
_____
_____
_____
_____
_____

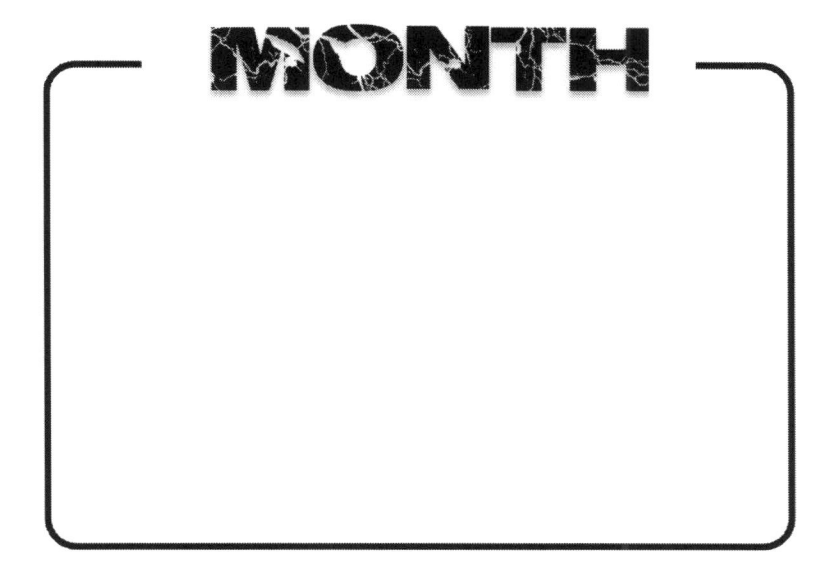

MONTH

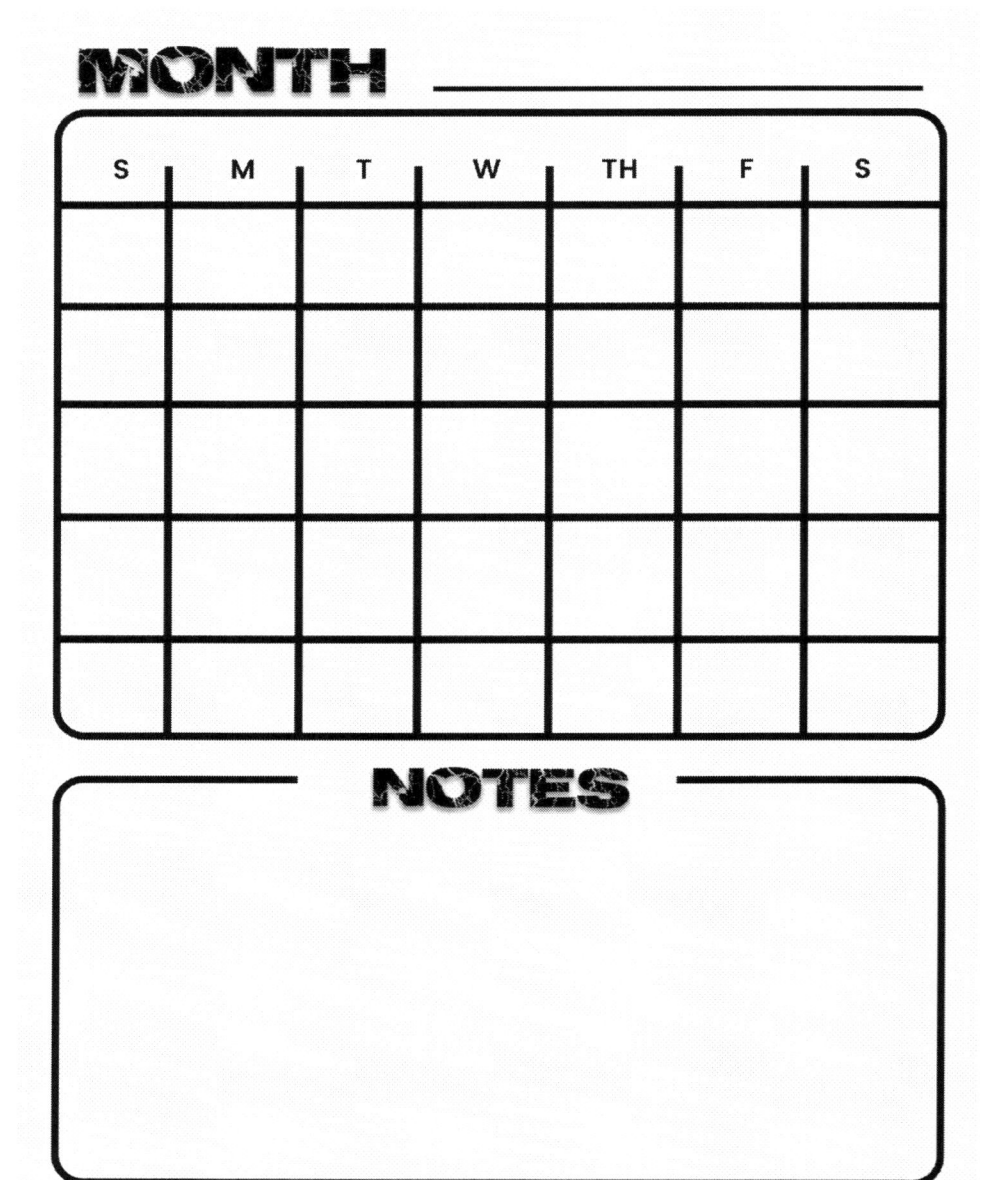

MONTH _____

S	M	T	W	TH	F	S

NOTES

THINGS TO DO THIS WEEK

MONDAY

___
___
___

TUESDAY

___
___
___

WEDNESDAY

___
___
___

THURSDAY

___
___
___

FRIDAY

SATURDAY

SUNDAY

PRAYER LIST

Chapter 10:
EXAMINE

"Examine what you tolerate. What you end up with is what you allowed. What you allow will definitely continue."

How can you analyze your process?

_____
_____
_____
_____

How can you acknowledge your progress?

_____
_____
_____
_____

How can you give attention?

_____
_____
_____
_____

WEEK 1

2 Corinthians 13:5 Examine your own selves, whether you are in the faith. Test your own selves. Or don't you know about your own selves, that Christ the Messiah is in you? Unless indeed you are disqualified.

Mediate and Write your thoughts about this scripture.

_____

_____

_____

_____

_____

_____

_____

_____

_____

_____

_____

_____

_____

THINGS TO DO THIS WEEK

MONDAY

TUESDAY

WEDNESDAY

THURSDAY

FRIDAY

SATURDAY

SUNDAY

PRAYER LIST

WEEK 2

Jeremiah 31:19 Surely, after that I was turned. I repented. After that, I was instructed. I struck high. I was ashamed, yes, even confounded, because I bore the reproach of my mouth.

Mediate and Write your thoughts about this scripture.

_____
_____
_____
_____
_____
_____
_____
_____
_____
_____
_____
_____
_____
_____
_____

THINGS TO DO THIS WEEK

MONDAY

___

___

___

TUESDAY

___

___

___

WEDNESDAY

___

___

___

THURSDAY

___

___

___

FRIDAY

SATURDAY

SUNDAY

PRAYER LIST

WEEK 3

Lamentations 3:40 Let us search and try our ways, and turn again to the Lord.

Mediate and Write your thoughts about this scripture.

THINGS TO DO THIS WEEK

MONDAY

_____
_____
_____
_____

TUESDAY

_____
_____
_____
_____

WEDNESDAY

_____
_____
_____
_____

THURSDAY

_____
_____
_____
_____

FRIDAY

SATURDAY

SUNDAY

PRAYER LIST

WEEK 4

Ezekiel 18:27-28 Again when the wicked man turns away from his wickedness that he has committed, and does that which is lawful and right he will save his soul.

Mediate and Write your thoughts about this scripture.

_____
_____
_____
_____
_____
_____
_____
_____
_____
_____
_____
_____
_____
_____
_____

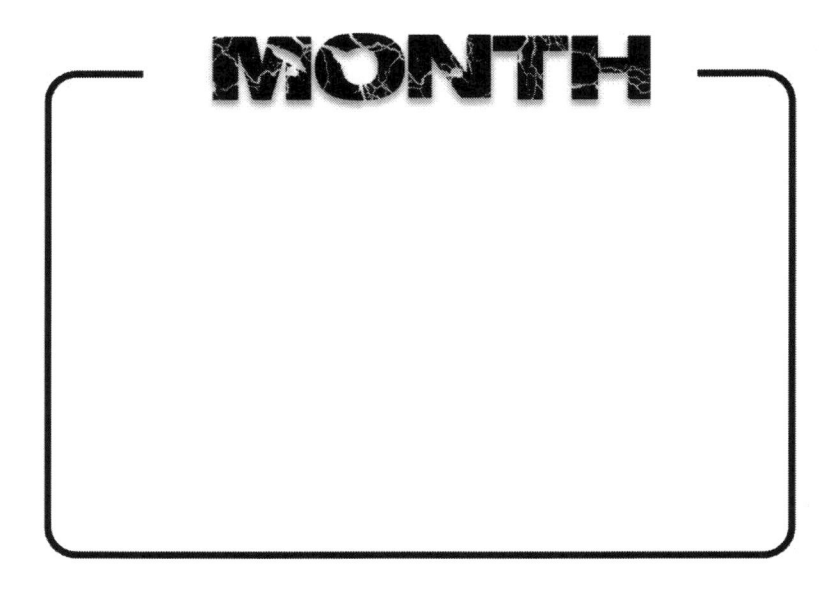

MONTH

MONTH _____

S	M	T	W	TH	F	S

NOTES

THINGS TO DO THIS WEEK

MONDAY

___

___

___

TUESDAY

___

___

___

WEDNESDAY

___

___

___

THURSDAY

___

___

___

FRIDAY

SATURDAY

SUNDAY

PRAYER LIST

Chapter 11:
KEEP MOVING
"Don't watch the clock, Do what it does, keep moving."

How can your beware of distractions?

_____
_____
_____

How can you push through fatigue?

_____
_____
_____

How can you not doubt yourself?

_____
_____
_____

How can you be your #1 motivator?

_____
_____
_____

WEEK 1

2 Corinthians 13:5 Examine your own selves, whether you are in the faith. Test your own selves. Or don't you know about your own selves, that Christ the Messiah is in you? Unless indeed you are disqualified.

Mediate and Write your thoughts about this scripture.

_____
_____
_____
_____
_____
_____
_____
_____
_____
_____
_____
_____
_____
_____

THINGS TO DO THIS WEEK

MONDAY

TUESDAY

WEDNESDAY

THURSDAY

FRIDAY

SATURDAY

SUNDAY

PRAYER LIST

WEEK 2

Job 17:9 Yet the righteous will hold to his way. He who has clean hands will grow stronger and stronger.

Mediate and Write your thoughts about this scripture.

_____
_____
_____
_____
_____
_____
_____
_____
_____
_____
_____
_____
_____

THINGS TO DO THIS WEEK

MONDAY

TUESDAY

WEDNESDAY

THURSDAY

FRIDAY

SATURDAY

SUNDAY

PRAYER LIST

WEEK 3

Philippians 3:14 I press on toward the goal for the prize of the high calling of God in Messiah Yeshua.

Mediate and Write your thoughts about this scripture.

THINGS TO DO THIS WEEK

MONDAY

TUESDAY

WEDNESDAY

THURSDAY

FRIDAY

SATURDAY

SUNDAY

PRAYER LIST

WEEK 4

Proverbs 4:18 But the path of the righteous is like the dawning light that shines more and more until the perfect day.

Mediate and Write your thoughts about this scripture.

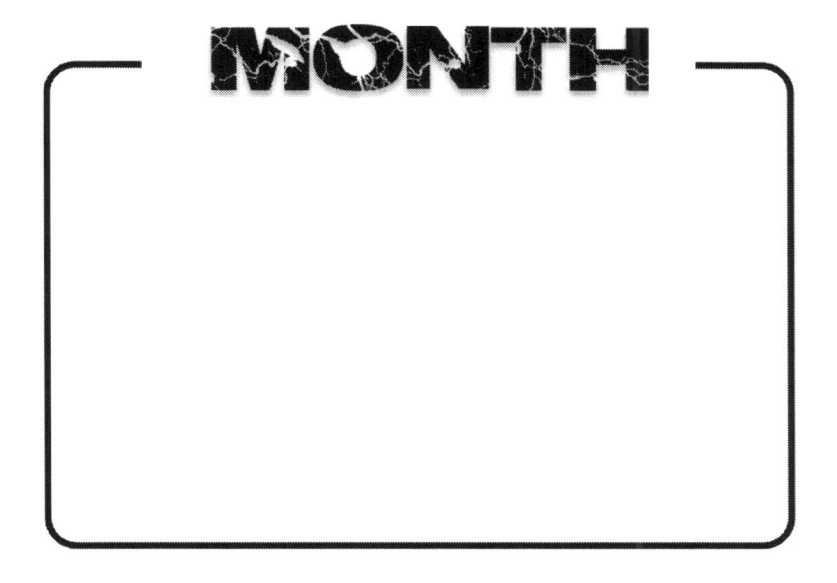

MONTH

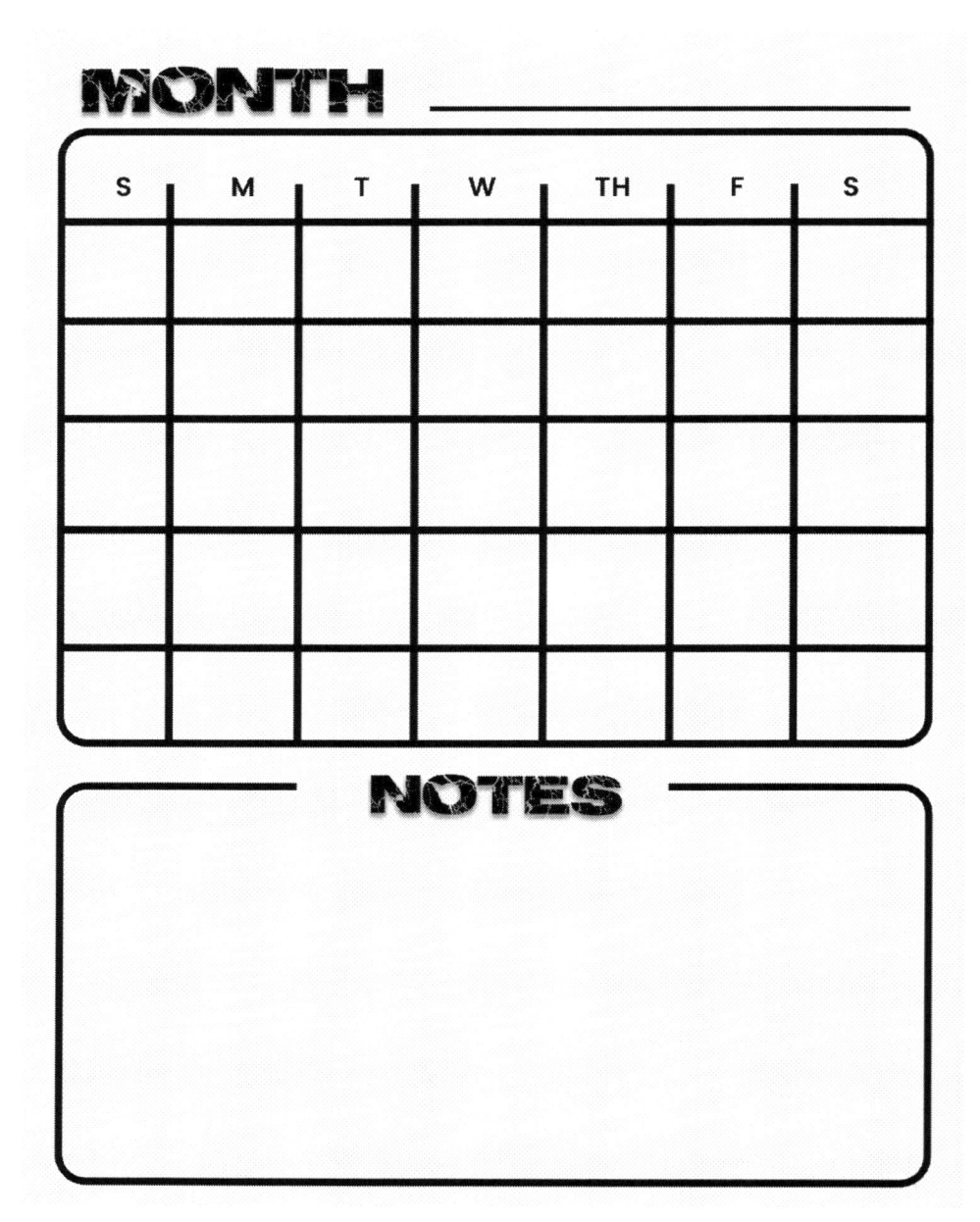

MONTH _____

S	M	T	W	TH	F	S

NOTES

THINGS TO DO THIS WEEK

MONDAY

TUESDAY

WEDNESDAY

THURSDAY

FRIDAY

SATURDAY

SUNDAY

PRAYER LIST

Chapter 12:
PERSEVERANCE
"Never stop fighting until you reach your divine destination, which is the unique YOU!"

How can you watch your thoughts?

_____

How can you start looking for the positive things?

_____

How can you avoid right/wrong dichotomies?

_____

How can you stop judging yourself?

_____

How can you focus on the now?

_____

How can you reverse your situation?

_____

WEEK 1

ROMANS 12:12 be joyful in hope, patient in affliction, faithful in prayer

Mediate and Write your thoughts about this scripture.

THINGS TO DO THIS WEEK

MONDAY

TUESDAY

WEDNESDAY

THURSDAY

FRIDAY

SATURDAY

SUNDAY

PRAYER LIST

WEEK 2

Colossians 1:11-12, 11 Being strengthened with all power according to his glorious might so that you may have great endurance and patience, 12 and giving joyful thanks to the Father, who has qualified you to share in the inheritance of his holy people in the kingdom of light.

Mediate and Write your thoughts about this scripture.

THINGS TO DO THIS WEEK

MONDAY

TUESDAY

WEDNESDAY

THURSDAY

FRIDAY

SATURDAY

SUNDAY

PRAYER LIST

WEEK 3

Galatian6:9 Let us not become weary in doing good, for at the proper time we will reap a harvest if we do not give up.

Mediate and Write your thoughts about this scripture.

THINGS TO DO THIS WEEK

MONDAY

_____
_____
_____

TUESDAY

_____
_____
_____

WEDNESDAY

_____
_____
_____

THURSDAY

_____
_____
_____

FRIDAY

SATURDAY

SUNDAY

PRAYER LIST

WEEK 4

James 1:12 Blessed is the one who perseveres under trial because, having stood the test, that person will receive the crown of life that the Lord has promised to those who love him.

Mediate and Write your thoughts about this scripture.

REFERENCES

New King James Version, Thomas Nelson 1979

Made in the USA
Columbia, SC
10 February 2020